Children with Privileges

Living in the Blessings of Romans 8

Rudolph A. Prescod

Copyright @ 2024 Rudolph Prescod

All rights reserved. No part of this book may be used or reproduced by any means, graphic, electronic, or mechanical, including photocopying, recording, taping or by any information storage retrieval system without the written permission of the author except in the case of brief quotations embodied in critical articles and reviews.

Books may be ordered through the author and Amazon.com

The views expressed in this work are solely those of the author and do not necessarily reflect the views of the publisher, and the publisher hereby disclaims any responsibility for them.

Cover concept: Rudolph Prescod
Cover design: Sheridan Frank, Frank Media Services
frankmedia592@gmail.com
Layout design: Denise Harris, DAH Publishing
dahpublishinggy@gmail.com

Join the
Children with Privileges Movement!

SCAN ME

*Share your testimony about the book.
*Ask questions. *Book an online or in
    *Post   person Group Study.
Prayer Requests.   *Order Books.
*Write a Review.

Call/WhatsApp: (USA) 419-771-0483; (GY) 592-685-3498
Email: prescool@yahoo.com

Table of Contents

Foreword   5

Acknowledgements   6

Introduction   7

1. Living Without Condemnation   11

2. Living the Life   22

3. Living as One Adopted   31

4. Living as Heir of the King   38

5. Living with Assistance in Prayer   45

6. Living in Providential Grace   53

7. Living in Everlasting Love   63

Go Live NOT Just Exist!   74

Foreword

On the walls of my office are canvas photos of several United States National Parks: Yellowstone, Yosemite, Grand Canyon, Tetons, and Denali. These were the most picturesque places on each trip. Some of these pictures I have seen in books and on the internet. However, they mean something special to me because I saw them "with my own eyes". Furthermore, I am reminded that it took considerable time to get to each of these locations.

The Epistle to the Romans is going somewhere. There are many locations along the way to "stop and look". However, nearly all would agree that Romans 8 is the pinnacle of the journey. From "no condemnation" in verse one to "no separation" in verse thirty-nine are awe-inspiring, magnificent, breath-taking "views".

In this book Rev. Rudolph Prescod is sharing the pictures he has taken from Romans 8. He has categorized these as "privileges" and "blessings". It was good for me to see again these magnificent truths through Rudy's lens. The questions at the end of each chapter are beneficial for consideration. Just as much they "slow us down" just enough to drink in the beauty we are seeing and in which we can live because of God's love for us. My hope for you in reading this book is that it will inspire you to go to Romans 8...and see for yourself....for the first time or again...all that we are and have in Christ Jesus our Lord.

Grace and Peace,

Rev. Geoff Kunselman
Former District Superintendent, Northwestern Ohio District,
Church of the Nazarene

Acknowledgements

This book is the culmination of many hours of toiling during the COVID-19 lockdown. I am grateful that God gave me the opportunity to be surrounded by my Toledo Trinity Church of the Nazarene and Chick-fil-A Toledo families who cared about my wellbeing as I quarantined.

I am grateful for my brother and colleague in ministry, Rev. Jared Burgess, for his invaluable time in content editing the manuscript; and my District Superintendent at the time of writing the script, Rev. Geoff Kunselman, for agreeing and taking the time to write the Foreword.

I must also acknowledge all the persons who have enquired of me and encouraged that I get another book published. Thank you for believing that there was something God has deposited in my spirit that needs to be penned.

Special thanks to my sister and friend of many years, Pastor Denise Harris of DAH Publishing who offered her skill and time to help me get this book published. Her offer was an answer to prayer and a true demonstration of the blessing of how God makes all things possible in His timing.

I close these acknowledgements with a high note of thanks and praise to Almighty God for His enabling power. Children with Privileges is about the privileges I enjoy as a son of God through faith in Jesus Christ.

Introduction

"Though I am the least deserving of all God's people, he graciously gave me the privilege of telling the Gentiles about the endless treasures available to them in Christ."

Ephesians 3:8 (New Living Translation)

Living in the blessings of the Christian experience is often challenging for most to navigate. The truth is, our fallenness as descendants of Adam and Eve has made it difficult for us to deal with the dynamic transition of our salvation experience; from death to life; darkness to light; and bondage to freedom. Truth be told, there is no easy way to disciple new believers into what it takes to be all that God has provided for us to be in Christ. It is also helpful to recognize that there is no "one size fits all" approach to navigating these challenges.

When Paul wrote to the Philippian believers, he said, **"Therefore, my beloved, as you have always obeyed, not as in my presence only, but now much more in my absence, work out your own salvation with fear and trembling; for it is God who works in you both to will and to do for His good pleasure"** (Philippians 2:12-13 New King James Version). The Apostle made it clear that our salvation experiences must be appropriated with an attitude that reflects an understanding of the serious effort it will take daily. However, he also states that the human effort is not without the supernatural workings of the same God who saves us. It is not in our strength alone but also by the Spirit. The Holy Spirit exhorts and enables.

The blessings of Romans 8 **(The Seven Privileges)** will be our focus in this book. The privileges are not just cliché terms of the Christian Faith, rather, they are attainable goals, realities which God has purposed for all His children to live and walk in daily as part of their born-again experience.

My hope is you are reading this book because of one of two reasons:

1. You know you are not living in the reality of these privileges daily, and you desire to do so.

2. You live in the reality of these privileges but want to examine if there is more that you can experience as a child of privilege.

Either of these two is an incredibly good reason for reading this book. Let me caution you however, that there is more God will say to you by His Spirit than I could have attempted to write in these pages. So, be open to the Spirit of God. He will use the limitations of these pages to take you into supernatural revelation and understanding of what He knows will help you live in the blessed privileges of Romans 8.

In Christ Jesus, **You are a child of privilege**! The reality of this life of privilege has nothing to do with any of your earthly realities like where you were born, or which family you were born into. Neither should this be made into another cliché statement. You are now **a child of privilege** because you have experienced new birth; you are born into the family of God. You now have the seal of God's Holy Spirit. You have all the rights the Bible says are afforded to children of the Almighty God. May God help you to understand that reality as you read and reflect.

So, what is a Privilege?

The definition I have chosen to use for this book is as follows: "a grant to an individual, corporation, etcetera, of a special right or immunity, under certain conditions." This definition uses two important words in the context of this book – 'individual' and 'corporation.' The word individual would of course refer to each individual child of God; each born-again disciple of Jesus Christ. The word corporation would be the reference to the Church as the corporate/universal Body of Believers.

This book discusses the seven privileges of Romans 8 like the definition states, as special rights and/or immunities which carry special spiritual conditionalities. This then behooves us to acknowledge that privileges require the recipients to take responsibility for committing to all the conditionalities which would qualify them to enjoy those privileges.

I challenge you to not settle for anything less than the awesome blessings afforded to every child of God. Let no one or anything dissuade you from pursuing what it means to live in the reality of these privileges.

This is a good time to read the entire eighth chapter of Romans a few times. Unless it is otherwise stated, I have used the New King James Version (NKJV) as the main reference for this book. I recommend you read the entire chapter (39 verses) for a broad overview of all it addresses.

Note that son/child/children will be used interchangeably to mean both males and females.

Chapter 1
Living Without Condemnation

Privilege #1 – Romans 8:1-9

Read these nine verses and keep in mind that the focus of this passage is the issue of freedom from condemnation. It will be useful to make a note of any words or phrases which address this issue directly or indirectly. Your personal notes will be beneficial as you read this chapter on privilege number one.

> "To be convinced in our hearts that we have forgiveness of sins and peace with God by grace alone is the hardest thing."
> *Martin Luther*

Living without condemnation may sound like a wild prospect to many. However, the scripture is clear in what it says and means. The damnatory sentence, the condemnation that all humans deserve, has been replaced with forgiveness and eternal hope.

The possibility and depth of this truth challenges the mind, especially when you think about the fact that a mindset of condemnation is often what the Christian can live with even though they are forgiven and freed from the power of sin. Yes, a mindset of condemnation can be an active part of the Christian's life even after they have repented of their sins, Jesus has taken His place of Lordship in their hearts, and they are active participants in the ministry or profession to which they believe God has called them.

While ignorance of what the scripture teaches about this truth may be a major factor, there are three likely reasons why the prospect of living without guilt would seem unlikely or even impossible to some.

1. **The mindset of condemnation can be self-imposed.**

    The believer can be greatly burdened by the darkness of their past to the point that it becomes difficult to not look back and be overwhelmed by that past. There may also be a struggle with a present besetting sin which serves as a huge challenge to living in victory. The heavy weight of guilt and shame can cause this self-imposition of guilt.

2. **The mindset of condemnation can be imposed by others.**

    A sad reality in the Christian community is the practice of some who use the sinful past or present struggles of others to keep them (steeped or bound) in guilt. Rather than use this as an opportunity to disciple and encourage growth, the struggling believer is held in bondage by scorn and is sometimes shunned. This kind of spiritual abuse can be inflicted innocently or intentionally. The victim can subsequently become trapped in guilt because the accuser is often a more 'mature' Christian for whom they have great respect.

3. The mindset of condemnation can be used by Satan as a weapon to hold one in bondage.

Satan could remind the Christian of their sins and use that to make that person question their salvation experience. He may also make the person question whether they are really forgiven and delivered. He can do this each time the person falls into sin and use these moments of failure and guilt to hold them in bondage. Jesus said it way, *"The thief does not come except to steal, and to kill, and to destroy…"* John 10:10a.

With these three possible stumbling blocks in mind, you must not allow yourself to be distracted from the awesome truth this scripture exposes. The depth of truth and reality which come with this first privilege impacts each of the other six. The child of God who is truly **Living Without Condemnation** is the one who can also enjoy the fullness of **Living the Life, Living as One Adopted, Living as Heir to the King, Living with Help to Pray, Living in Providential Grace,** and **Living in Everlasting Love**. You are one of those children of privilege.

Reality Check

"There is therefore now no condemnation to those who are in Christ Jesus,..." v. 1a

The preceding seven chapters of Romans give evidence of the human predicament. They highlight the weakness of the human nature to respond adequately to the Law rightly and thereby address that predicament, and the redemptive work of Christ which was and still is the only way for humans to live above sin. Romans 7:24 and 25 sum it up this way, ***"O wretched man that I am! Who will deliver me from this body of death? I thank God---through Jesus Christ our Lord!"***

The Word of God states that it is the will of God that you walk free of any condemnation, and this is directly connected to your relationship with Christ Jesus. As a child of God, the privilege is extended to you to walk free from the burden of condemnation. This is a precious gift from God.

Being a child of God excludes you from having to live daily in the mindset of condemnation sin brings. This reality has both present and futuristic implications. The Greek word used for condemnation denotes that you have been set free from the damnatory sentence which is prepared for those who remain in the life of sin. This means you are delivered from the daily condemnation you may live with as a burden to your soul. It also means you are free from the future condemnation which excludes you from heaven and damns you to an eternal hell. One responsibility you have is to learn how to appropriate the reality of this privilege with the help of the Holy Spirit.

Another responsibility that is critical to realizing this privilege is to understand that spiritual blessings come with conditionalities. The beauty is, God places the weight of these conditionalities on your dependence upon Him. You must learn to trust His Word and His Spirit.

The Conditionality

"...who do not walk according to the flesh, but according to the Spirit" v. 1b

The major conditionality of this privilege is your commitment to a daily resistance of the works of the flesh. The flesh affects you negatively because of your inherited fallenness/lostness. Your salvation experience has provided forgiveness of your personal sins, but it is the deeper work of the Holy Spirit which cleanses and frees you from the bondage of inherited sin. The call is for a very deliberate commitment to resisting all the works of the flesh in and by the power of God's Spirit.

The scripture makes it noticeably clear that to live in the reality of this privilege you must commit to a life of submission to the leading of the Holy Spirit. Paul the Apostle says it this way, ***"I have been crucified with Christ; it is no longer I who live, but Christ lives in me; and the life which I now live in the flesh I live by faith in the Son of God, who loved me and gave Himself for me"*** (Galatians 2:20). The Holy Spirit is the "third person" of the triune Godhead; the One who has come to be the life of Christ in and through the Christian. The life-giving and empowering Spirit of God is He who makes this privilege real.

Undoubtedly, this conditionality cannot be adhered to by mere human effort. There must be complete dependence upon the enabling power of the Holy Spirit. You should be encouraged that He is your ever-present help.

The Greater Law

"For the law of the Spirit of life in Christ Jesus has made me free from the law of sin and death" v. 2.

The conditionality of this privilege can be met because there is a new law in place. There are a few key characteristics of this new and greater law of which you must be aware.

1. The Holy Spirit is the source of the life you now have in Christ Jesus. The old law was written on stone and was weak and limited. It was purely by human effort that the old law was followed. The law of the Spirit, the new law, is written on the hearts of humans, on your heart. This new law is powerful and has unlimited potential because the Spirit is resident in your heart and serves as the teacher, enabler, and guide when you submit to Him.

2. You have been made free from the law of sin and death. You are now set free to live above sin in the present and escape eternal separation from God in the future. The law of the Spirit has liberated you from the inherited, fallen nature of Adam. The life of holiness is possible because God has provided the remedy through the cleansing, infilling, empowering work of the Holy Spirit. You no longer must be a slave to sin in word, thought, or deed.

3. You do not have to pursue a righteousness which comes from human effort. You are now the righteousness of God in Christ. Paul said it this way to the Church at Corinth. *"For He made Him who knew no sin to be sin for us, that we might become the righteousness of God in Him"* (2 Corinthians 5:21). God gave the gift of His own Son that He would condemn sin in the flesh for the children of God.

4. The renewing of your mind is essential as the carnal mind is focused only on things of the flesh. *"For to be carnally minded is death, but to be spiritually minded is life and peace"* v. 6. Because of how the carnal mind impedes one's ability to have a meaningful spiritual walk, the Spirit of Christ guarantees the transformation needed by the renewing of the mind of the believer. *"And do not be conformed to this world, but be transformed by the renewing of your mind, that you may prove what is that good and acceptable and perfect will of God"* (Romans 12:2). The law of sin and death is broken and rendered ineffective as the believer submits to the Spirit of life.

5. You have been sealed with the Holy Spirit. Like the authenticating seal on a manufactured product, the Holy Spirit serves as the seal on the heart and soul of the child of God. You carry the seal of heaven. God recognizes you as His own and *"The Spirit Himself bears witness with our spirit that we are children of God"* (Romans 8:16). Once you bear the seal of the Spirit it is your privilege to experience all that God has provided for those who choose each moment of each day to be His children through relationship with Jesus Christ.

Because of the Spirit who dwells in you, and who enables and empowers you, there is now the depth of spirit to walk in the awesome victory of life without condemnation. Paul admonished the Church at Ephesus this way.

Living in the Reality of Privilege #1

At the root of freedom from condemnation is your cleansing from that fallen nature which you inherited from Adam. God frees those who confess their sins and believe that the salvific work of Jesus the Christ is the only provision for receiving this freedom from condemnation. The evidence of this freedom is a life lived in the power of the Spirit. The child of God who benefits most from this privilege is the one who lives committed to being led by the Spirit of God in every waking moment of each day.

You are now free to live a victorious life as a child of God. There is no need to submit to a self-imposed mindset of condemnation. There is no need to submit to a mindset of condemnation imposed by others. There is no need to submit to a mindset of condemnation from the pit of hell. This is a privilege that you are entitled to enjoy as a disciple of Jesus Christ if you are faithful to the required conditions. Living in the reality of this privilege lays the solid foundation needed to live in the other privileges. You are now free from the power of indwelling sin and the Spirit of God lives in you.

> *"Grace and peace be multiplied to you in the knowledge of God and of Jesus our Lord, as His divine power has given to us all things that pertain to life and godliness, through the*

knowledge of Him who called us by glory and virtue, by which have given to us exceedingly great and precious promises, that through these you may be partakers of the divine nature, having escaped the corruption that is in the world through lust" (2 Peter 1:2-4).

I encourage you to take some time to respond to the reflection questions for this chapter. This should help create some momentum as you get to the reflection questions in the following chapters. You may also use the spaces provided to write your responses.

Questions for Reflection

1. What has been your experience with the issue of condemnation and how has this chapter spoken to your reality?

_____
_____
_____
_____
_____
_____
_____
_____

2. In what area of your life do you think there is the most need for listening and sensitivity to the leading of the Holy Spirit?

_____
_____
_____
_____
_____
_____
_____
_____

3. Where are you in relation to living in the law of the Spirit today? Think of your response in relation to what the life of holiness looks like in scripture.

_____
_____
_____
_____
_____
_____
_____
_____

4. Is there at least one thing this chapter has opened in your heart and mind? If yes, please share.

_____
_____
_____
_____
_____
_____
_____
_____

Chapter 2
Living the Life

Privilege #2 - Romans 8:10 – 11

Read these two verses and keep in mind that the focus of this passage is the issue of what it means to have eternal life. It will be useful to make a note of any words or phrases which address this issue directly or indirectly. Your personal notes will be beneficial as you read this chapter on privilege number two.

> "I have seen (as far as it can be seen) many persons changed in a moment from the spirit of horror, fear, and despair to the spirit of hope, joy, peace; and from sinful desires, till then reigning over them, to a pure desire of doing the will of God."
>
> *John Wesley*

Living without the bondage of condemnation has opened the door for you to genuinely experience the power of the incarnate Christ in your mortal body.

However, there is the challenge of seeking to live in this newness of life you have in Christ against the pull of the flesh. This challenge highlights the need for you to trust the Spirit to do a work which will make this privilege a reality in your daily walk.

The abiding presence of the Spirit of Christ and the life which has come to your dead body and soul is the essence of the second privilege. The second part of John 3:16 says this, *"...whoever believes in Him should not perish but have everlasting life."* This verse makes direct reference to the work of Christ through the cross and the life you now live as a blessed privilege. This second privilege is the **LIFE** which only the Spirit can give.

The Strong's Lexicon defines this everlasting life as, "life real and genuine, a life active and vigorous, devoted to God, blessed, in the portion even in this world of those who put their trust in Christ, but after the resurrection to be consummated by new accessions (among them a more perfect body), and to last forever."

This privilege means you now have the amazing opportunity to live the life which Adam and Eve enjoyed before the fall; right relationship with God, right relationship with each other, and right relationship with the rest of creation through cleansing from the fallen, inherited nature. This is the quality of life, everlasting life, which God has provided in and through Jesus and it is good for time and eternity.

Reality Check

"And if Christ is in you, the body is dead because of sin, but the Spirit is life because of righteousness" v. 10.

The implication here is that the presence of the Spirit of Christ in your body does not change the fact that the physical body is going to die because of sin. The human body is destined for the grave. This does not mean your body is not precious. However, the Spirit gives life to the soul that lives in right relationship with Christ. The living soul then lives a righteous life in the body. Here are Paul's words to the church at Corinth. ***"Do you not know that you are the temple of God and that the Spirit of God dwells in you? If anyone defiles the temple of God, God will destroy him. For the temple of God is holy, which temple you are"*** (1 Corinthians 3:16-17).

While we will never escape many of the effects of the fallen nature as we walk this earth, this second privilege allows the believer to live in the righteousness of God in and through Christ Jesus. You have the privilege of walking victoriously every moment of each day in the new life which only the Spirit gives.

The Promise

"...He who raised Christ from the dead will also give life to your mortal bodies through His Spirit who dwells in you" v. 11b.

This is a promise which speaks to the awesome work God says He will do in the life of all those who will allow His Spirit to have the preeminence in their mortal bodies.

Firstly, in the first part of this eleventh verse, God promises He will do this miraculous work by the same Spirit who raised Christ from the dead. Remember this, God does not make promises and not keep them. ***"The Lord is not slack concerning His promise, as some count slackness, but is longsuffering toward us,..."*** (2 Peter 3:9). However, is it not mind-blowing that the same dynamic power by which Christ was raised from the dead is now at work in your feeble mortal body? Only the Spirit can help you understand and appreciate the depth of this truth. The awesome God wants you to live in the power of this promise. The gift of life is now yours because the life-giving Spirit dwells in you.

Secondly, God says He will do this work from the inside out. His Spirit will dwell in you and will give life to your mortal body. God's promise is you will have the power to honor Him by the power of the Spirit from within. God has made the provision for the power of sin to be broken in the body. You can now live above sin. The quality of life, the holy life, can now be realized because the Spirit who makes it possible dwells in you. In his writing to the saints at Galatia about not returning to the Law; the written code, he says, ***"I have been crucified with Christ, it is no longer I who live, but Christ lives in me; and the life which I now live by faith in the Son of God, who loved me and gave Himself for me"*** (Galatians 2:20).

If the Spirit of Christ truly dwells in you, this promise is your new reality. The promise has been fulfilled in your life. You are now able to live the dynamic life the Spirit gives.

Living in the Reality of Privilege #2

The awesome God of heaven has chosen to dwell in the hearts of humans. If this does not leave you in awestruck wonder, I invite you to stop and consider the depth of this reality. Who are we that God should choose to reside in us by His Spirit? *"But one testified in a certain place, saying: 'What is man that You are mindful of him, or the son of man that You take care of him?'"* (Heb. 2:6 [Job 7:17; 15:14; Psa. 8:4; 144:3]). God wants His glory to be seen in and through us. As we walk in the newness of life He gives, we serve as living examples of what His life can look like to others if they trust Him.

God has made it possible for you to have life in your fallen mortal body by the same power by which He raised Christ from the dead. The Holy Spirit is the Third Person of the Triune Godhead who empowers every child of God. Unlike those who lived under the law, you are not tied to a written moral code. You are now called to live in submission to the Holy Spirit who dwells in you.

To teach new Gentile converts, Paul wrote these words to the Church at Thessalonica. *"Now may the God of peace Himself sanctify you completely; and may your whole spirit, soul, and body be preserved blameless at the coming of our Lord Jesus Christ"* (1 Thessalonians 5:23). Paul highlights the need for the sanctifying work of the Spirit. By the power of the Spirit, the soul is cleansed from inherited depravity. By that same power, the spirit is quickened to be responsive to the things of God. As a result, the body is made alive; it is given the ability to live in submission to the leading of the Holy Spirit on the spirit and soul.

This is a dynamic life in comparison to the former life of bondage and defeat. You have been given the privilege of walking in the power of the life-giving Holy Spirit.

I am certain the time you took to respond to the reflection questions at the end of the first chapter was worth it. Ask the Spirit to help you and use the spaces provided to write your responses to this next set of questions.

Questions for Reflection

1. What notable difference/s have you or others seen in the spiritual direction and quality of your life?

2. What has been your experience as it relates to the sanctifying work of the Holy Spirit in your heart and life?

3. Is there an area of your life which still must be completely surrendered to the Holy Spirit, and what is that specific area?

_____
_____
_____
_____
_____
_____
_____
_____

4. If the response to the previous question is identifiable, how do you plan to address it?

_____
_____
_____
_____
_____
_____
_____
_____

5. Is there at least one thing this chapter has opened in your heart and mind? If yes, please share.

_____
_____
_____
_____
_____
_____
_____
_____

Chapter 3

Living as One Adopted

Privilege #3 - Romans 8:12 - 16

As you read these verses, take the time to focus on adoption as a unique opportunity for the disadvantaged and disenfranchised to be given the sense of belonging, love, and security a family provides. God has chosen to adopt the redeemed as His children.

> "If anybody understands God's order for his children, it's someone who has rescued an orphan from despair, for that is what God has done for us. God has adopted you. God sought you, found you, signed the papers and took you home."
>
> *Max Lucado*

Now that you have a better understanding of the first two privileges, it is time to examine the privilege of adoption. In most cultures around the world, this is a normal legal practice which allows many, especially young children, the opportunity to be accepted and incorporated into a family other than their own. This legal process allows them the privilege of carrying the name of the adopting family and access to the rights and privileges that their new family share.

Paul wrote about adoption to the Church at Galatia as a spiritual blessing for all the redeemed. He said,

"But when the fullness of time had come, God sent forth His Son, born of a woman, born under the law, to redeem those who were under the law, that we might receive the adoption as sons. And because you are sons, God has sent forth the Spirit of His Son into your hearts, crying out, 'Abba, Father!' Therefore you are no longer a slave but a son, and if a son, then an heir of God through Christ" (Galatians 4:4-7).

He also wrote in the first chapter of his letter to the Church at Ephesus about the spiritual blessings the saints have in Christ. He writes about the blessing of adoption as follows, ***"... having predestined us to adoption as sons by Jesus Christ to Himself, according to the good pleasure of His will, ..."*** (Ephesians 1:5). It is God's good pleasure to welcome you into His family, as a legitimate child. The privilege of adoption is given to all who come to God through Christ, without any consideration of their former social or spiritual familial realities.

What an awesome thing that the family of God is so diverse in its makeup, and He loves us all the same. He paid for our adoption with the blood of His Son.

The Conditionality

"For as many as are led by the Spirit of God, these are the sons of God" v.14.

Like the major conditionality of the first privilege and the promise of the second, this one requires your commitment to the daily leading of God's Spirit. Writing to the Romans, Paul establishes that we are now debtors and thereby expected to commit to living according to the Spirit. For to be led by the Spirit of God is a defining mark of those who are sons. If you are truly a son of God by adoption, then it cannot be just to enjoy the earthly temporal blessings and privileges. This must also be evidenced by your commitment to the responsibilities that come with sonship.

Submission to the leadership of the Holy Spirit is one of the major themes of this eighth chapter of Romans. God has shifted the focus from the Law to the Spirit. The Spirit is the person of the Godhead who plays a major role in the conviction, conversion, and consecration of every human who comes into adoption. There should be evidence of consistent and not occasional submission to the leading of the Spirit in the life of every child of God.

The Right to say Abba

The Holy Spirit has given you the right to use the proper title for Father, Abba, when speaking to God. You do not need to feel intimidated when approaching God in prayer. The bondage of intimidation has been nullified by the Spirit of adoption. To this the Spirit bears witness. You now can approach His throne with reverence and enjoy the awesome privilege of confessing openly that you are a legitimate child of God. Your Father does not see you as anything but a joint heir with Christ His Son. You are not treated differently because of your adoption.

The Father expects you to refer to Him as Abba. His purpose is to relate to you in an intimately personal way. He also has purposed to bring you into every spiritual blessing as an heir with Christ, including your glorification with Him at the last day.

Living in the Reality of Privilege #3

God the Father has gifted you with the privilege of being His child. Learning to live as a son or daughter may at times seem like a daunting prospect. However, it is helpful to recall that anything God expects or requires of you He comes alongside to help you accomplish it. The Holy Spirit, the divine Paraclete is the One who does this.

This kind of relationship is only realized as an authentic daily reality in and through the presence and power of the Holy Spirit. You must learn to recognize the Spirit's voice and respond in obedience to His prompting. There must be a sensitivity to the leading of the Spirit in all spheres of your life. Paul wrote to the Church about the possibility of stifling or suppressing the Spirit. He said very simply, ***"Do not quench the Spirit"*** (1 Thessalonians 5:19). Your submission to the Spirit is critical to you living in victory over sin in your heart and life, the way God has purposed for all His children to do.

By now the reflection questions should be proving to be most useful as you reflect on how the reading is speaking to you personally. Continue to trust the Spirit to help you and use the spaces provided to write your responses to this next set of questions.

Questions for Reflection

1. How significant is the concept of God as Father to you?

2. What are some of the ways adoption/sonship has added value to your life in comparison to what it was before?

3. How does your daily walk testify to others that you are a Spirit led Child of God?

___

4. Are there ways you may have quenched the Spirit, and if yes, examine why and what you need to do to avoid repeating these actions?

___

5. Is there at least one thing this chapter has opened in your heart and mind? If yes, please share.

_____
_____
_____
_____
_____
_____
_____
_____
_____

Chapter 4
Living as an Heir of The King

Privilege #4 - Romans 8:17 - 25

While we continue to absorb the blessing of adoption into the family of God, the reality that we are heirs of the King of kings is a concept which requires our full attention in order to grasp its substance and depth. This King is ruler of a kingdom that is different from and greater than all earthly kingdoms combined.

> "Think of what you are, you Christians. You are God's children; you are joint heirs with Christ. The 'many mansions' are for you; the palms and harps of the glorified are for you. You have a share in all that Christ has and is and shall be."
>
> *Charles Spurgeon*

Learning to live in the depth of this privilege will require that the child of God be clear about the nature of this King and the Kingdom over which He rules. There is much said throughout scripture about God as King.

The King about whom we speak is thus described. ***"For the LORD Most High is awesome; He is a great King over all the earth"*** (Psalm 47:2). This great and awesome King has chosen to make Himself known to you and has done everything necessary for you to have relationship with Him, as His child. By the privilege of adoption, you are made an heir to the King of kings. The psalmist says, ***"The LORD has established His throne in heaven, and His kingdom rules over all"*** (Psalm 103:19). You are heir to the King who said *"...Heaven is My throne, and earth is My footstool..."* (Isaiah 66:1).

Everything this King is and owns is available to you now and for eternity. Another important element is that God has not shown favoritism when it comes to who become heirs or how they are treated. James used the demonstration of personal favoritism by the believers to remind them of this. After pointing out their partiality, he said to them, ***"Listen, my beloved brethren: Has God not chosen the poor of this world to be rich in faith and heirs of the kingdom which He promised to those who love Him?"*** (James 2:5). The children of the King are expected to behave like their Father. Therefore, partiality cannot be part of the behaviors which are practiced in the family. We must all be grateful that Abba has made us heirs.

Reality Check
"For I consider that the sufferings of this present time are not worthy to be compared with the glory which shall be revealed in us" v. 18.

This is a Kingdom of suffering and glory. Being heir to this King is not only about the glitter and cool experiences which accompany royalty. You have also been given the privilege of identifying with the sufferings of Jesus. These sufferings will vary in scope and severity for each child of God. However, it is one of the painful honors you must experience as an heir. The One with whom you are a joint-heir, Jesus, had to bear many sufferings during His time on earth. Fortunately for us, this has allowed Him to identify with us as humans in our times of suffering. It also means that He can come to our aid during those difficult times.

On the flip side of suffering there is the incomparable glory which will be revealed when the heirs stand before the King. Here is what the Hebrew letter says, *"For it was fitting for Him, for whom are all things and by whom are all things, in bringing many sons to glory, to make the captain of their salvation perfect through sufferings"* (Hebrews 2:10). God has this unique way of making something beautiful come out of ashes. He created our intricate bodies out of the dust of the earth. Now here He has promised an incomparable glory out of suffering. I like how Peter says it when he wrote about our heavenly inheritance.

> *"In this you greatly rejoice, though now for a little while, if need be, you have been grieved by various trials, that the genuineness of your faith, being much more precious than gold that perishes, though it is tested by fire, may be found to praise, honor, and glory at the revelation of Jesus Christ"* (1 Peter 1:6-7).

There is no way of escaping suffering and trials, but they can in no way be compared to the glorious presence our God and King.

Our Hope

"But if we hope for what we do not see, we eagerly wait for it with perseverance" v. 25.

Try to imagine the excitement of waiting for something you have been promised and hope to have, maybe a gift for your birthday or Christmas. Your eagerness to wait rests in the confidence you have in the one who made the promise. You have no doubt this person will keep their word. So you wait with great patience because of hope.

This hope, this blessed hope you now have, rests in Christ's ultimate work of the redemption of your body. You are called to believe that this hope is real because it is the hope into which you were saved. The Apostle Peter says, ***"Blessed be the God and Father of our Lord Jesus Christ, who according to His abundant mercy has begotten us again to a living hope through the resurrection of Jesus Christ from the dead"*** (1 Peter 1:3). You can be confident that the consummation of this hope is as sure as Jesus was raised from the dead. You can look forward in anticipation that your faith is not in vain.

The scripture admonishes, ***"…that having been justified by His grace we should become heirs according to the hope of eternal life"*** (Titus 3:7). You and every other heir of the King is challenged to persevere to the end. You are called to demonstrate a determination and commitment to wait patiently and faithfully to inherit this hope, even in the face of suffering and trials. The glorious appearing of this hope will be much greater.

Living in the Reality of Privilege #4

God wants you to walk in the blessing of this privilege and receive all that is prepared for the heirs of His kingdom. However, it should be clear that you must be prepared to walk in the sufferings which come with the journey. There is no shortcut to the blessing of being an heir. Neither is there any special favor which will exclude any from having to identify with the suffering of Christ.

you to walk in the blessing of this privilege and receive all that is prepared for the heirs of His kingdom. However, it should be clear that you must be prepared to walk in the sufferings which come with the journey. There is no shortcut to the blessing of being an heir. Neither is there any special favor which will exclude any from having to identify with the suffering of Christ.

Sometimes it will require a double portion of grace to make this privilege bearable. Nonetheless, it is total dependence on the Spirit that will make patience a welcome virtue. You will not have to walk alone. The Spirit of God is in you and beside you and it is by His strength you will walk as an heir.

Do not allow yourself to be distracted. A high price was paid to bring you into the Kingdom. There is too much at stake. Hold on and ask God to help you live one moment at a time, one day at a time, until He comes.

You are now challenged to respond to the reflection questions at the end of the fourth chapter, "Living as an Heir of the King." The Holy Spirit is faithful to continue helping you write your responses to this set of questions. Lean on Him!

Questions for Reflection

1. What does being an heir of God's Kingdom mean for you in the context of having to identify with the suffering of Christ?

___

2. How would you explain to someone how having a living hope makes a difference in how you live?

___

3. Is there at least one thing this chapter has opened in your heart and mind? If yes, please share.

_____
_____
_____
_____
_____
_____
_____

Chapter 5
Living with Assistance in Prayer

Privilege #5 - Romans 8:26 - 27

Prayer is the privilege we have of personal communication with the One who is Abba. As you reflect on this, please give much thought to how much this changes the dynamic of our relationship with the God of heaven. Share in the personal and corporate privilege called prayer.

> "Prayer involves transformed passions. In prayer, real prayer, we begin to think God's thoughts after Him: to desire the things He desires, to love the things He loves, to will the things He wills."
>
> *Richard J. Foster*

Are you ready for this? This privilege gives us direct communication with the God who is creator and sustainer of the universe. We can talk with the awesome God about anything at any time. Because communication is not a one-way street, we also get to listen to Him as He speaks to us.

In this privilege you will develop one of the most intimate spiritual disciplines. Here you will communicate with the God who has a personal interest in everything concerning your life. The King about whom we have already learned so much, desires to have face to face interaction with you. This great and awesome God has chosen to give you opportunity to learn and recognize His voice. He wants to make Himself known to you in a relationship which He has initiated through the gifts of His Son and Spirit.

Reality Check

"Likewise the Spirit also helps in our weaknesses. For we do not know what we should pray for as we ought, but the Spirit Himself makes intercession for us..." (Romans 8:26a).

There should be no shame in us admitting we need help to pray. Truth is, we often do not know what to say and how we should pray. Prayer gives us the awesome privilege of communicating with the God who is omniscient, and only the Spirit of God can assist us in our weakness as we pray. I encourage you to be like the disciples of Jesus who said to Jesus, *"...Lord, teach us to pray, as John also taught His disciples"* (Luke 11:1). Jesus' response to His disciples was intended to help them in their weakness. His model for them is now ours by extension. The major elements of Jesus' model point us to some of the ways we can trust the Spirit to assist us as we pray.

The prayer model from Jesus serves mostly as a guide and says:

> ***"Our Father in heaven,"*** – Acknowledge God for who He is as the exalted One.
>
> ***"Hallowed be Your name."*** – Magnify His holy and exalted name.
>
> ***"Your kingdom come."*** – Ask for His rulership to be real on the earth.
>
> ***"Your will be done on earth as it is in heaven."*** – Ask for His perfect will to be evident in the hearts and lives of humans.
>
> ***"Give us day by day our daily bread."*** – Acknowledge Him as our source of daily Sustenance.
>
> ***"And forgive us our sins,"*** – Repent and seek forgiveness for personal and corporate sins.
>
> ***"For we also forgive everyone who is indebted to us."*** – Ask for the grace and strength to forgive others.
>
> ***"And do not lead us into temptation but deliver us from the evil one."*** – Acknowledge God as the only One who can lead away from temptation and the evil one. (Luke 11:2-4).

Even in this limited human model you can trust the Spirit to direct you in specific models of prayer. The last part of the Romans 8:26 verse says, *"...but the Spirit Himself makes intercession for us with groanings which cannot be uttered."*

This privilege allows us to be recipients of the Spirit's intercession on our behalf. When our weakness hinders us in prayer, the Spirit intercedes with groanings which only God can understand. You can pray with the liberty in your own spirit that the Holy Spirit will be faithful in the times when you are weak. This should keep you humble as you pray. It should also help you to approach prayer with the confidence that you are not alone. The Spirit is there to assist you when you do not know how and what to pray.

Divine Accuracy in Prayer

"Now He who searches the hearts knows what the mind of the Spirit is, because He makes intercession for the saints according to the will of God" (Romans 8:27).

Jesus the great High Priest is directly involved in helping you as you pray. Since He focuses on our hearts and not our eloquence, He is able to make intercession on your behalf. He who searches your heart, also knows the mind of the Spirit and the perfect will of God. He alone can understand and confirm how these align with each other.

Therefore, many have been able to testify of being led to pray for someone at a time when they had no way of knowing what that person was experiencing. Yet later it was confirmed that the way they were led to pray was exactly the right time and right prayer for what the other person was going through. The Spirit who knows all things can direct in ways which transcend time and distance. All God asks is that we trust and obey. As the Spirit directs you to pray and it seems 'strange' and uncomfortable, you must trust that He will never mislead you. Often His intention is not just for the benefit of other person who is being prayed for, rather, it is for the one praying to learn and grow in the practice of this privilege.

The other fascinating thing is that the Son of God, who knows the perfect will of God for us personally and corporately, makes intercession for us before the Father. Romans 8:34 confirms that Jesus is the One *"...who is even at the right hand of God, who also makes intercession for us."* Is it not a huge blessing to know that there are times when we are not even engaged in prayer, and the Son is faithful to intercede on our behalf? Have you come to the place in your walk with Christ where you trust Him to know exactly what is perfect for you to pray at that time?

Living in the Reality of Privilege #5

This privilege requires every child of God to work on developing the discipline needed for this privilege to be a meaningful part of their spiritual journey.

We have established yet again that you learning to lean heavily on the wisdom and guidance of the Spirit is key to this privilege being most beneficial. It is also important that you be prepared to acknowledge when you do not know how and what to pray. The Spirit will be faithful to assist. It is kind of paradoxical that acknowledging weakness in this regard is considered being strong. Most importantly, however, is the need to never forget that the Lord knows all things and can be trusted to assist us and make intercession for us with great accuracy. The Spirit and the Son make intercession for us. We are blessed!

I encourage you to respond to these reflection questions prayerfully. The Spirit is He who will enable you to hear the heart and mind of God as you reflect and plan on the way forward. Take as much time as you need to respond meaningfully.

Questions for Reflection

1. How have you dealt with acknowledging weakness when engaging in the spiritual discipline and privilege called prayer?

_____
_____
_____
_____
_____
_____
_____

2. What are some of the things you have done to develop a prayer-life routine?

3. Do you have an example of at least one time when you knew the Spirit was directing you to pray a certain way and you did not fully understand why?

4. Is there an area of challenge you have had in your prayer-life and were able to overcome? Share what it was and how you overcame.

_____
_____
_____
_____
_____
_____
_____
_____

5. Is there at least one thing this chapter has opened in your heart and mind? If yes, please share.

_____
_____
_____
_____
_____
_____
_____
_____

Chapter 6
Living in Providential Grace

Privilege #6 - Romans 8:28 - 30

These three verses are powerful because they take you into the providential grace of God. Reflect on the realities of what it looks like to live with God in control of every situation and outcome in your life. This privilege allows you to face the realities of life with the knowledge that God's only agenda is what is good for you.

> "If God has made your cup sweet, drink it with grace; if He has made it bitter, drink it in communion with Him. If the providential will of God means a hard and difficult time for you, *go through it.*"
>
> *Oswald Chambers*

While God's providential grace is a very real part of who He is, it also serves as a point of contention to some. This is so because when our life experiences have painful experiences and/or outcomes the following questions may be asked, "If God is all powerful, why didn't He stop this from happening?" "If God is love, why does He allow bad things to happen to good people?" "What good could ever come out of this disaster?" Our theology instructs us that God does not cause these painful experiences and outcomes, but He sometimes allows them for our good and His good purpose. So, what does it take to live in the confidence that this awesome God will cause all my experiences, my 'THINGS,' to have both temporal and eternal value and benefit for me?

It is a privilege to have the awesome God in control of everything concerning our lives. We can live with the confidence that God's providential grace is always at work on our behalf. This means that even when there are 'THINGS' we are not comfortable with, have no control over, or which we cannot understand why they are happening to us, we can trust that the omnipresent, omniscient and omnipotent God is fully aware and in control. We must believe that nothing concerning us catches Him by surprise. The scripture also admonishes us that there are certain kinds of gifts we can expect to receive at God's hand. *"Every good gift and every perfect gift is from above, and comes down from the Father of lights, with whom there is no variation or shadow of turning"* (James 1:7).

Reality Check #1

"And we know that all things work together for good..." Romans 8:28a

Being a child of God, does not exclude us from life's challenging 'THINGS.' The truth is, there may be persons who believe that their faith in the salvific work of Christ should and could exclude them from the many painful 'THINGS' which are part of the human experience. Paul says we already know this exclusion from challenging 'THINGS' is not true. The emphasis in this verse is on *'all things.'* How do we know that all things work together for good? There are three possible ways we may come by this knowledge.

1. Through the Word of God, the Bible.

There are numerous examples throughout the Old and New Testaments of how God has worked in the lives of His children individually and corporately by using a combination of 'things.'

2. Through our own experiences.

We could miss this because of how much we are overwhelmed by the experiences themselves. However, this is one way by which we know the validity of this truth.

3. Through the experiences of other believers.

The saints whose testimonies we get to hear also serve us well. These saints are our contemporaries who have lived in the reality of seeing their 'THINGS' work together for good.

As we reflect on these three ways by which we come to this knowledge, there are two truths we must note about who God is. First, He is the God of purpose. He does nothing in the earth or in our lives personally and corporately without purpose in mind. Second, He works supernaturally to influence all things as He wills. There is nothing that happens in the life of a child of God that did not first get His attention and approval/disapproval. The account of Job serves as an excellent example of this.

Reality Check #2

All things are NOT painful

Thankfully, not all the 'THINGS' in our lives are challenging and painful. There is so much that God allows us to experience that is pleasant and joyous. Sometimes it would seem as though these good 'THINGS' get overshadowed by the darkness and pain of the challenging ones. This may have been your experience at different times.

You may have wished that you could have all favorable experiences, but that does not seem practical in real life.

Reality Check #3

God can be trusted with all things

We have trained ourselves to focus on our realities, the 'THINGS' only as individual experiences and not as ones connected for our good.

A huge part of your challenge is to see your experiences together and not as individual roads that do not intersect. If this is done, then you can appreciate that He takes all your experiences and works them together for your good. It is kind of like mixing the ingredients on a recipe. They are all so different in texture, taste, smell, nutritional value (or lack thereof), and the amounts needed, yet when we work them together as the recipe instructs, the outcome is good.

In this instance, God is asking you to trust Him to be the "Master Chef" of sorts. He is asking you to believe that because of who He is, He can and will make your 'THINGS' work together for good. Therefore, it is not your place to try figuring out how He will do this but to trust Him and believe that He will. Trusting God's providential grace is an awesome privilege which allows us to learn so many things about 'His ways.'

If you have not proven Him yet, I encourage you to trust His providential grace.

Those Who Love God

While God's providence is often manifest in the lives of those who are not identified as His children, the promise in this scripture is relationally specific. This then begs the question, "Who are those that love God?" These are the persons who have firstly, responded to the love of God in and through Christ. ***"For you are all sons of God through faith in Christ Jesus"*** (Galatians 3:26). Secondly, the lovers of God are a people who have responded to God's love through total consecration. This is how Jesus said this consecration must be expressed. ***"…You shall love the LORD your God with all your heart, with all your soul, with all your strength, and with all your mind, and your neighbor as yourself"*** (Luke 10:27). It was also stated earlier in the chapter on the third privilege, *"For as many as are led by the Spirit of God, these are sons of God"* (Romans 8:14). Those who are identified as lovers of God are guaranteed they will enjoy the benefits of this privilege.

Those Who are the Called According to His Purpose

Transformation is the goal

Remember, we established that He is the God of purpose. He does nothing without purpose. Whatever God allows in our lives, especially when it is not by our own choosing, it is because He knows it will have immeasurable benefit for us for time and eternity. God knows all of these 'THINGS' are designed to bring us *"...to be confirmed to the image of His Son..."* (Romans 8:29b). God's purpose is to transform us and bring us into Christlikeness.

In Romans 12, verses 1and 2, Paul admonishes the Church to present their bodies as living sacrifices and resist confirming to that which is worldly, that which John describes as the *"...lust of the flesh, the lust of the eyes, and the pride of life-..."* (1 John 2:16). These actions are to be taken so that like the Church at Rome you could *"...be transformed by the renewing of your mind, that you may prove what is that good and acceptable and perfect will of God"* (Romans 12:2).

Paul also admonished the Philippian Church to be like Christ. He said to them, *"Let this mind be in you which was also in Christ Jesus,..."* (Philippians 2:5). God's providential grace is intended to bring us more into the image and likeness of His Son. This was His original plan in the Garden. Adam and Eve possessed this likeness before they disobeyed God. The privilege is now yours to be confirmed to the image of the Son by the sanctifying, transformational work of the Spirit.

The Called, the Justified, the Glorified

God calls all humans unto Himself. Peter confirms God's intention for us when he wrote, *"The Lord is not slack concerning His promise, as some count slackness, but is longsuffering toward us, not willing that any should perish but that all should come to repentance"* (2 Peter 3:9). God predetermined that those who respond to His call through repentance, He will make them righteous in Christ, and those made righteous will also be made worthy (Romans 8:30).

If you are numbered among those who love God, you have the assurance that God wants to do this good work in you by His Spirit. God has worked everything out before time began. This was so important to God that He set it all in motion before the foundations of the earth were laid. As a child of privilege, God's purpose for you is beautiful. He is making all 'THINGS' work together for your good. That one good is to do His cleansing, sanctifying work in your heart and bring you into the image of His Son.

Living in the Reality of Privilege #6

While the focus here is on God's providence, there are so many of the elements of the previous five privileges which are wrapped up in this one. I pray that God will help you to be deliberate about how you grow and live in the reality of this privilege.

Learning to see God as working all things together for your good will require that you get closer to Him. This will be especially true when you encounter those THINGS which are painful. You can only learn to trust Him as much as you get to know Him. You can only love Him as much as you get to understand the depth of His love for you. You can only see His purpose accomplished in your life as much as you get to know Him as the God of purpose. Job understood this when he said, ***"You gave me life and showed me kindness, and in your providence watched over my spirit"*** (Job 10:12 New International Version). Even in his most difficult circumstances, Job knew he could trust God's providential grace.

Just like Job, you can learn to trust God's providence. Like all the other privileges, living in God's providential grace can be your daily reality.

By now you should see how responding to the reflection questions is proving to be worth completing before moving on with your reading. If the spaces provided are not adequate, write or type your responses somewhere else where you can retrieve them easily.

Questions for Reflection

1. How have you dealt with accepting the providence of God in your life, especially when you could not understand how all things would work together for good?

   _____
   _____
   _____
   _____
   _____
   _____
   _____
   _____

2. Share an experience which you now recognize as the outcome of many things which God worked together on your behalf.

   _____
   _____
   _____
   _____
   _____
   _____
   _____
   _____

3. Is there at least one thing this chapter has opened in your heart and mind? If yes, please share.

_____

_____

_____

_____

_____

_____

_____

Chapter 7
Living in Everlasting Love

Privilege #7 - Romans 8:31 - 39

God is love! God loves unconditionally. As you examine what this privilege means in your life as a child of God, I encourage you to pay attention to how this passage talks about how this love is expressed by God.

> "Though our feelings come and go, His love for us does not. It is not wearied by our sins or our indifference; and therefore, it is quite relentless in its determination that we shall be cured of those sins at whatever cost to us, and at whatever cost to Him."
>
> *C.S. Lewis*

Everything we can understand about God as He has revealed Himself to us, is wrapped in the attribute that He is love. God does not just demonstrate love; the very essence of His nature is love. Everything the triune God thinks, says, and does flows out of this love. This is the main reason God loves unconditionally; He is love in His essential nature. The eternal God loves eternally. It is the expression of His love that has brought you into the reality of these seven privileges, and the greatest of them is love.

What an awesome privilege to not only be loved by God but to also live in the reality of that love each day as you walk in all the other privileges. His everlasting love will be with you for time and eternity.

At this point in the passage, the writer seeks to bring the discourse on privileges to a close with a few questions. This was a method of teaching Jesus used often during His ministry. His questions were not intended to gather information, rather, they were always for the benefit of the respondents, to help them learn some spiritual truth. Let us see how these seven (7) questions will help you come into more truth.

Significant Questions Privilege Poses

Question 1

"*What then shall we say to these things?*" Romans 8:31a

The one thing you should want to say to these things, these privileges, is *'thank you God for your love which has graciously brought the riches of heaven to a wretch like me. You did not exclude me because of what men may use to exclude me from their temporal earthly privileges.'* I will let you decide if there is anything else you may want to say.

The God of purpose has been very intentional about ensuring these kingdom privileges are highlighted and made to be understood as superior to any earthly privileges you may or may not ever enjoy. Earlier in Romans the writer said this, **"Because of our faith, Christ has brought us into this place of undeserved privilege where we now stand, and we confidently and joyfully look forward to sharing God's glory"** (Romans 5:2). There is so much that can be said as we testify about the benefits of these privileges.

Question 2

"If God is for us, who can be against us?" v. 31b

This question is not meant to suggest that as child of God no one will come against you. Rather, it highlights how fruitless it is for anyone to even consider coming against you. Here is what He promised in Isaiah 54:17, **"No weapon formed against you shall prosper, and every tongue which rises against you in judgment you shall condemn. This is the heritage of the servants of the LORD, and their righteousness is from Me, says the LORD."**

If God is for you, everyone who comes against you will have to deal with Him. Abba, your Father, has made numerous promises regarding your well-being. God has given His angels charge over you. The blood of Jesus also serves as a cover and protection against the attacks of Satan. These privileges in your life are proof that God is for you and will defend you against the wiles of the devil and any person who will seek to harm you.

Question 3

"He who did not spare His own Son, but delivered Him for us all, how shall He not with Him also freely give us all things?" v. 32.

The deduction here is that since God freely gave His best gift, His Son who came as the sacrifice for your sin, what else is of greater significance that He would withhold from you. In and through His Son, God has made His kingdom accessible to His children. God's will is that all who put their trust in Jesus would walk in the fullness of what newness of life in Him means. He gives all spiritual blessings to His children freely.

Here is what Paul wrote to the Corinthian Church. ***"Now we have received, not the spirit of the world, but the Spirit who is from God, that we might know the things that have been freely given to us by God"*** (1 Corinthians 2:12). There is no need for you to live in ignorance of all the things God has for you in Christ Jesus.

Question 4

"Who shall bring a charge against God's elect?" v. 33.

Again, this question is not meant to suggest that as a child of God no one will bring a charge against you. The writer posits a response to this question by pointing out how meaningless a charge will be because it is God who justifies. You are justified in Christ. This means two things:

i. Jesus is representing you before the Father,

ii. The charge is null and void because it is already under the blood of Jesus.

God's everlasting love will not leave you hopeless. In the parable of the persistent widow the question is asked, *"And shall God not avenge His own elect who cry out day and night to Him, though He bears long with them?"* (Luke 18:7). God's seemingly delayed timing does not mean He has neglected His own. Whenever a charge is brought against you, Jesus is your lawyer and priest and will represent you well before the Father.

Question 5

Who is he who condemns? v. 34a.

The first privilege addresses this question directly. The pronoun 'who' may mean one of three persons – You, Others, or Satan. In the light of what God has done for you through Jesus Christ, none of these persons have the authority to condemn you. We have already established that there is *"…no condemnation to those who are in Christ Jesus, who do not walk according to the flesh, but according to the Spirit."*

Condemnation is a thing of the past because you now live in the victory of the New Covenant. You have been saved and sanctified and the Spirit of God is the One whose voice you obey as you walk by faith in the Son of God.

Question 6

Who shall separate us from the love of Christ? v. 35a.

It is said you should not answer a question with a question, but I would like to break that rule. Who is the person with the authority to separate you from the love of Christ? Who will you allow to separate you from the love of Christ? Any person you allow to do this, has immediately become your god. To have someone separate you from the love of Christ is to declare the love of God demonstrated through Christs' sacrifice as null and void.

The love of Jesus Christ for you could not be demonstrated anymore clearly. So, here is my final question. If Christ has let His love be seen and experienced by you in such amazing ways, who shall separate you from this love?

Question 7

Shall Tribulation, or distress, or persecution, or famine, or nakedness, or peril, or sword? v. 35b.

This question addresses the 'what' that shall separate you from the love of Christ. While this is not an exhaustive list, it covers a wide range of things which can possibly seek to accomplish this goal. Remember, God may allow you to experience some of these 'things' but His providential grace will cause them to work together for your good.

There is too great a cloud of witnesses who have gone before you from whose examples you can learn and draw strength. These witnesses, these heroes of the faith, have shown that it is possible to come through and not be separated from the love of Christ. You do not have to succumb to any hardship because you are not alone. You are a child of victory. You are a child of privilege who is walking in His everlasting love.

Reality Check

"For Your sake we are killed all day long; we are accounted as sheep for the slaughter" v. 36.

The writer reminds us that part of our reality in Christ is that we are living sacrifices. To make this point he quotes Psalm 44:22. This is one of the ways we identify with Jesus. We identify with His suffering. We have already established that the privileges do not all come without some measure of sacrifice and pain for us sometimes. If you contribute to a theological position which teaches of a painless spiritual journey, I recommend you reexamine the origins of that school of thought.

While you are considering the level of commitment it takes to be a living sacrifice. The writer goes on to point out that sacrifice does not mean defeat. Amid all the things which may attempt to separate you from the love of Christ, you are more than a conqueror (v. 37), and this, in and through the everlasting love of Christ.

In verses 38 and 39, he states very emphatically that none of the things listed there will be able to **"...*separate us from the love of God which is in Christ Jesus our Lord.*"** Listen to how the Apostle Paul talks about this to the young Timothy. ***"Therefore, do not be ashamed of the testimony of our Lord, nor of me His prisoner, but share with me in the sufferings for the gospel according to the power of God, ..."*** (2 Timothy 1:8). Paul talks about suffering for the gospel as an honorable thing which you accept without shame.

The everlasting love of God elicits a loving response from those who are true disciples, the children of privilege.

Living in the Reality of Privilege #7

Living in God's everlasting love must bring us into two transformational experiences. The first one has to do with our loving response to God. 1 John 4:19 says, *"We love Him because He first loved us."* This must be the natural response to the everlasting, unconditional love of God. He deserves our love and He does enable us to love Him by the power of His Spirit. The second one has to do with our relationship with others. Here is what the scripture says about our relationship with others. *"If someone says, 'I love God,' and hates his brother, he is a liar; for he who does not love his brother whom he has seen, how can he love God whom he has not seen?"* (1 John 4:20).

God's desire is for His everlasting love to flow in and through the life of each of His children. You cannot be a child of privilege and just be a recipient of this awesome, everlasting love. This privilege challenges us to be those through whom the love of God will flow to others. *"Dear friends, since God so loved us, we also ought to love one another"* (1 John 4:11). This love cannot be counterfeited. This privilege allows you to experience the deepest level of what it means to be like Christ.

To have the blessing of this privilege is to then have this same love be the testimony to who you are and whose you are. Paul's letter to the Corinthian Church elaborates on the significance of this love. 1 Corinthians 13 is often referred to as the great love chapter. A life which demonstrates the love of God in these ways is only possible *"...because the love of God is shed abroad in our hearts by the Holy Ghost which is given unto us"* (Romans 5:5).

This is a life you have been given the privilege of walking in by the power of the life-giving Holy Spirit. The everlasting love of God is alive in you so let your life of privilege be seen by your unconditional love for others.

You have made it to the end of the seventh chapter. Now you are about to respond to the final set of questions. Let the Holy Spirit lead you as you reflect on how He has spoken to your heart concerning this seventh privilege.

Questions for Reflection

1. What has been most significant about the love of God for you?

_____
_____
_____
_____
_____
_____
_____

2. Which of the seven Significant Questions Privilege Poses did you learn the most from?

_____
_____
_____
_____
_____
_____
_____
_____

3. Is there anyone you must ask God to teach you to love? If your response is YES, what will you commit to doing for God to teach you by His Spirit?

_____
_____
_____
_____
_____
_____
_____
_____

4. Is there at least one thing this chapter has opened in your heart and mind? If yes, please share.

_____
_____
_____
_____
_____
_____
_____
_____

Go Live NOT Just Exist!

> "Most of all, God has blessed us by giving us the privilege of knowing Him and walking with Him every day. He did this by sending His Son into the world to die for our sins."
>
> *Billy Graham*

    Now that you have gone through the seven privileges, my hope is that this book has challenged and inspired you to ensure you are in the place a child of privilege needs to be before God. This place of privilege is God's gift to you. You do not have to be ashamed nor afraid to tell anyone about this because it did not come easily. However, it is also important to not be arrogant about it either. Living as God's child of privilege must be an attractive lifestyle, not repulsive. Its attractiveness will be the quality-of-life God gives; life lived above the mere temporal, earthly privileges so many choose. If you are one who lives with some exclusive earthly privileges, this book says to you, the privileges of the heavenly kingdom supersede all your earthly ones.

    The dynamic, exciting life experienced in being a disciple of Jesus Christ is something that can only be understood and appreciated when someone submits to it. I trust you have been able to see how these privileges are interrelated and touch so many other blessings and areas of your spiritual walk. Despite all your challenges past, present, or future, God has called you to live in a way that contradicts mere human existence. You have received the dynamic life of the Spirit...You are not just existing! You are experiencing some of what it means for God's kingdom to be in the earth as it is in heaven (Matt. 6:10; Luke 11:2). The rulership of God in your heart and access to the rights and benefits of the kingdom should cause others to recognize that you have privileges they do not have.

Here is a challenge and a promise Jesus will always state to us when we may be tempted to be overly worried about our temporal needs; what we will eat, drink, and wear. He says, ***"But seek first the kingdom of God and His righteousness, and all these things shall be added to you"*** (Matthew 6:33). Jesus understands that we can be distracted from what is important. He is most concerned about your spiritual sustenance. He also understands your struggle to walk in righteousness but has made a way for you to walk in these privileges victoriously.

The challenges of the seventh chapter of Romans are real. However, the child of God is called to live in the privileges of chapter eight (8) as he/she remains connected to the Father through Jesus. Romans 8 has given you seven privileges that are yours as you remain in relationship with Jesus the Christ and obey His Spirit. You have the privilege of:

Living without Condemnation

Living the Life

Living as One Adopted

Living as Heir to the King

Living with Assistance to Pray

Living in Providential Grace

Living in Everlasting Love

The ways that these will work out in your daily experiences is not for me to attempt to explain; that would be an exercise in futility. However, you can LIVE with the confidence that the God who has spoken these things does not lie. Neither is He slack concerning His promises.

> *"But you are a chosen generation, a royal priesthood, a holy nation, His own special people, that you may proclaim the praises of Him who called you out of darkness into His marvelous light; who once were not a people but are now the people of God, who had not obtained mercy but now have obtained mercy"* (1 Peter 2:9-10).

You are a child of privilege. May God help you to walk victoriously in that reality for the rest of your earthly sojourn.

My personal points of Reflection

My personal points of Reflection

My personal points of Reflection

My personal points of Reflection

Citations

Page 9 – https://www.dictionary.com/browse/privilege

Page 11 – Martin Luther. (n.d.). AZQuotes.com. Retrieved May 06, 2020, from AZQuotes.com Web site: https://www.azquotes.com/author/9142-Martin_Luther

Page 22 – John Wesley Quotes. (n.d.). BrainyQuote.com. Retrieved June 15, 2020, from BrainyQuote.com Web site: https://www.brainyquote.com/quotes/john_wesley_789619

Page 31 – Max Lucado (2011). *"The Great House of God"*, p.15, Thomas Nelson Inc.

Page 38 – https://www.christianity.com/wiki/bible/what-bible-mean-children-of-god.html

Page 45 – Richard J. Foster (1995*). "Richard Foster's treasury of Christian discipline", Jossey-Bass

Page 53 – https://utmost.org/updated/the-supreme-climb/

Page 63 – Lewis, C. S. (2012). *Mere Christianity*. p. 133, William Collins.

Page 74 – Billy Graham. (n.d.). AZQuotes.com. Retrieved May 10, 2020, from AZQuotes.com Web site: https://www.azquotes.com/quote/779515

Made in the USA
Middletown, DE
13 July 2024